ONE WORD DEVOTIONAL FOR YOUNG ADULTS

A PRACTICAL YET SPIRITUAL APPROACH TO LIFE

[Henry L Johnson III]

DEDICATION

This Devotional Is Dedicated To The Young Adults In My Life: Sons And Daughters, Matthew (Cortney), Mark (Heather), Blandon (Pam), Annetta, Langston, Murdock, And To All Young Adults.

Table of Contents

INTRODUCTION 6

CHAPTER-1 8

Depression 8

I King 19..............................8

CHAPTER-2 13

Forgiveness............................13

Genesis 41:50-52 13

Psalms 103: 12.................13

CHAPTER-3 18

Purpose 18

Jeremiah 29:11.................18

CHAPTER-4 22

Pride.......................................22

Philippians 2:1-3...............22

CHAPTER-5 25

Temptation.............................25

1 Corinthians 10:13 25

CHAPTER-6 30

Laugher 30

Proverbs 17:22.................30

CHAPTER-7 33

Successful 33

John 4:30-34.....................33

CHAPTER-8 36

Romans 8:35-39....................36

CHAPTER-9 40

Acts 4:34-37 40

CHAPTER-10 43

Mentorship 43

1 John 2:14.......................43

CHAPTER-11 46

Philippians 4:6-7 46

CHAPTER-12 53

Conformity 53

Philippians 4:8 54

CHAPTER-13 56

Confidence 56

2 Corinthians 1:9-10.........56

CHAPTER-14 60

Patience..................................60

Isaiah 40:31.......................60

CHAPTER-15 63

Grateful 63

CHAPTER-16 66

Finances 66

Psalms 24:1 66

CHAPTER-17 70

Addiction 70

Genesis 9:19-21 70

John 5 70

CHAPTER-18 73

Regret....................................73

Psalms 51 73

CHAPTER-19 77

Friends.....77

Proverbs 18:24.....77

CHAPTER-20..... 81

Thoughtfulness.....81

Philippians 2:3.....81

CHAPTER-21..... 84

Children.....84

Psalm 127:3-5 ESV.....84

CHAPTER-22..... 88

Mask.....88

Exodus 34:33.....88

Exodus 34:33-35.....88

CHAPTER-23..... 91

COVID.....91

Isaiah 53:5.....91

2 Chronicles 7:14.....92

INTRODUCTION

Someone said, "if you want to make God laugh, just show Him your plans." Life is such a complicated and complex spectrum. There are so many diversities of social life and marital life. Yet, there must be consistency and relevancy so young adults can retain their bearings. Juggling school, student loans, occupation, children, bills, mortgage, babysitting, and so many more.

That is why this one-word devotional is such a vital entity. First, it brings daily routine into the life of the young adult. Each day they may read something that could affect their entire day with bits of joy, praise, and understanding.

Secondly, it helps young adults anticipate daily biblical encouragement and wisdom.

I found in my life that a one-word devotional is so helpful, and it is easy to remember. The scriptures say:

12 For the word of God is alive and active. Sharper than any double-edged sword, it penetrates even to dividing soul and spirit, joints and marrow; it judges the thoughts and attitudes of the heart. (Hebrews 4:12) KJV.

Hoping this one-word devotional becomes a valuable part of your spiritual life. Would you buy this book and leave a review?

God Bless,

Author

CHAPTER-1

Depression

I King 19

19 And Ahab told Jezebel all that Elijah had done and how he had slain all the prophets with the sword.

2 Then Jezebel sent a messenger unto Elijah, saying, So let the gods do to me, and more if I make not thy life as the life of one of them by tomorrow about this time.

3 And when he saw that, he arose, went for his life, and came to Beersheba, which belongs to Judah, and left his servant there.

4 But he went a day's journey into the wilderness, and came and sat down under a juniper tree: and he requested for himself that he might die; and said, it is enough; now, O Lord, take away my life; for I am not better than my fathers.

We begin our devotional with a low note, depression. Most would not want to talk about this part of life, yet it plagues our mental capacity. That melancholy feeling of sadness and a loss of interest in activities causes impairment of daily life.

This could become a prolonged period in the life of individuals.

I am not a doctor; therefore, I can only give practical precepts and examples from the Word of God to help you in your situations. However, I would suggest you seek your physician's help if what I described as a definition of depression is affecting your behavior.

In this scripture, it appears the great prophet Elijah has reached a point of depression. You might ask, “How could this be? This prophet spends his waking hours consulting with God?” He has performed many miracles and presented many signs and wonders, two of which are numerous. He began by cutting off the rain because of a wicked king Ahab whose wife was Jezebel, both idol worshipers. Then Elijah saved a widow and his son by miraculously producing meals for bread during the famine. Then he confronts King Ahab and his prophets in Mt Carmel. God rules and causes the false prophets to be destroyed. When Jezebel found out what happened, she threatened to take Elijah’s life.

It appeared as if Elijah had had enough and began a journey away from the Queen, Jezebel. We pick up in I Kings chapter 9, where we see a depressed prophet. We see fear as he tries to get away from the Queen, we see a traveling schedule that includes over 35 miles from Judah to Beersheba, and he went a distance from that point a day's journey, which would include at least another 15 miles for a total of over 5o miles (v3,4).

What symptoms did the prophet display? Anxiety, suicidal tendencies, a feeling of worthlessness, loneliness, as if no one has experienced his depression. Elijah said, take my life, Lord! Am I any better than my father? His fathers did not take their lives, and others took their lives.

What are some of the keys to limiting depression, using Elijah's life as a model:

1. Rest (v 5-7) It helps to recoup mental health, increases mental capacity, helps to build immunity to all kinds of diseases, reduces stress, gives better metabolism, and increases a healthy attitude.
2. Eat (v 5-8) nourishment and strength
3. Communion with God (our prayers keep us in touch with heaven)

4. A reset mindset (v 10) Elijah told the Lord he was the only true prophet left to face the monarchy. Sometimes our depression puts us in a category all to ourselves as we ponder our condition, not realizing that it may not be as bad as we think.
5. Purposeful activities (V 15-18) Activity with a purpose, not just something to do, but finding something to do that interests you and those you are helping.
6. Finding someone to mentor (v 19-21) Ask the Lord to help you find someone within your profession that needs mentoring. The more we concentrate on others, the less we concentrate on ourselves.
7. Learn to praise God for the results in your life.

Prayer

Lord, sometimes I wish this cloud of sadness would just go away. I have no energy to do what I should do around the house. I am fearful of so many things; I am afraid of Covid, how it has ravished families and friends, and I am afraid for my children with these school shootings, bullying, and strange friends. I am afraid I do not have enough funds to meet my needs. However, I am not afraid of you, lord. Will you take away my cloud of sadness and turn it into gladness? Will you give me more strength to carry out my daily activities? Will you clear my mind so I can understand and function properly? I truly thank you in advance. I praise you, In the name of Jesus (Amen)

CHAPTER-2

Forgiveness

Genesis 41:50-52

Psalms 103: 12

[12] As far as the east is from the west, so far hath he removed our transgressions from us. (Amnesia and Ambrosia)

[50] And unto Joseph were born two sons before the years of famine came, which Asenath, the daughter of Potipherah priest of On bare unto him.

[51] And Joseph called the name of the firstborn Manasseh: For God, said he, hath made me forget all my toil and all my father's house.

[52] And the name of the second called he Ephraim: For God hath caused me to be fruitful in the land of my affliction.

I will never forgive him for what he did to me! I will never forgive her for what she did to me! We are now divorced, and I will never forgive them. She had an affair, he had an affair, and I will make her pay. That boss treated me badly, and I won't forget it. He robbed me of my money in the stock market, and I will never forgive this mess.

We could go on another 2 hours over the myriad of things that deserve not to be forgiven. But today, I want to share a man who had the right not to forgive his brothers but to forgive them.

Yes, Joseph in the Bible was afflicted! He had the right to be angry. He was taken away from his family and sold into slavery at 17. In Egypt, he had to learn another nation's language and culture. Joseph was placed in the home of the Captain of the Guards (Potiphar). In a few months, he became the chief steward in the household. Potiphar's wife wanted Joseph all to herself. But Joseph had integrity and tried to stay away from her. She brought false charges to her husband. Potiphar placed Joseph in Jail, but the Lord was with him. Joseph interpreted dreams for Pharoah's Butler, and he was returned to Pharoah's palace, but he interpreted the baker's dream, and it came true; the baker lost his life. Pharoah had a dream interpreted by Joseph that saved the entire world from a 7-year famine. Pharoah showed Joseph his appreciation by making him second only to Pharoah. He also gave Joseph his wife. They had two sons:

50 And unto Joseph were born two sons before the years of famine came, which Asenath, the daughter of Potipherah priest of On bare unto him.

51 And Joseph called the name of the firstborn Manasseh: For God, said he, hath made me forget all my toil and all my father's house.

52 And the name of the second called he Ephraim: For God hath caused me to be fruitful in the land of my affliction.

Here's the key Joseph leaves us after his afflictions; he is now 30 years old, after 13 years of affliction, and a crucial time in a teenager's life. He gives his sons meaningful names. Manasseh (Amnesia), the Lord helped him to forget all the toil he had to go through that came from his father's house. It could have destroyed his health and mind if he did not forgive. He had willful amnesia; he chose to forget. We must choose to forget those mean and hateful gestures on the part of others. It left his mind, he didn't say, "I forgive, but I won't forget." Joseph said, "I forgive, and I forget.

His other son Ephraim (Ambrosia), the Lord, caused me to be fruitful in the land of my affliction. A pleasant aroma permeated the atmosphere of Joseph. He forgot what was done to him, and he was fruitful in the land of his affliction. How could he be so content with what happened to him?

Joseph realized, as we must, that nothing can occur except it comes from the Lord. And if it comes by Him, there must be a reason! And it will work out for my good because He has a plan I cannot see.

Ultimately, his brothers were terrified that Joseph was still alive and that he was second to Pharoah. Next, they were petrified that they had to return to Egypt a second time. Finally, they were mortified that Joseph sat them in the dining hall according to their ages, (Only someone who knew Jewish culture could do such a thing.

The final summation for Joseph to his brothers: "You meant it for evil, but God meant it for Good.

Psalms 103:12 mentions as far as the east is to the west, so far has he removed our sins

The psalmist did not say as far as the North to the South, so far has he removed our sins? You see, our God can remove all our sins, and He was not interested in the measurements of the North and South because we can measure North and

South, but east and west cannot be measured. So if we travel to the east, we will end up in the west without measure. So let's develop the kind of forgiveness our Lord has for us.

Prayer

Lord, sometimes what is done to me is so egregious that I become angry just thinking about it. It hurts when this happens, and it is hard for me to forget, let alone forgive. I believe Joseph's story has helped me see the kind of forgiveness needed in my case. I do know not only Joseph forgave his brothers, but there is another one who showed the entire world how to forgive when he went to Calvary and died on the cross; he said, "Father, forgive them, for they know not what they do!" I need your spirit to help me to free myself from this heavy burden and release my mind from carrying this waste of time and energy. Thank you, Lord, for what you will do in my life (Amen).

CHAPTER-3

Purpose

Jeremiah 29:11

New International Version

11 For I know the plans I have for you," declares the Lord, "plans to prosper you and not to harm you, plans to give you hope and a future.

Growing up on the east side of Akron, Ohio, in a two-bedroom house with 6 other brothers and sisters, the only thing on my mind at that time was going to school, playing sports, and going to church. I had no idea what my future appeared to be. I know to honor and respect my parents and try not to do anything that would bring embarrassment to the family.

While growing up, I saw several little signs of what the Lord wanted out of my life; the Lord gave me the ability to sing, the music director auditioned me at Robinson Elementary school, and I became a member of the school choir. I also was allowed to sing a solo on our church broadcast. Later, my two brothers and I, along with one of my sisters, became known as the Johnson singers. We sang at churches, and when my dad pastored a church, we were his choir.

Later in life, I was given another indication from the Lord at my high school graduation. My high school class asked me to give the closing prayer at our graduation.

Now, after Pastoring for over 44 years, along with singing many songs, I am retired from Pastoring with a Doctor of Divinity degree. After many nights of studying and hundreds of sermons written, my soul has become a believer from a young man who could not speak or review the Sunday school lesson on Sunday morning.

The Lord was faithful to me, and he will be faithful to you.

I want you to think about some of the signs the Lord has already given you about your life. You know what they are, but you have ignored them because they didn't seem to fit your lifestyle or the friends you associate with. You are afraid your friends might disapprove of your choices. I want you to know that it is better to aim for the Lord's approval than for your friends.

The scripture says: "I know the plans I have for you." That means one person knows your future, and He used the term "Plans In the earlier years of going to the movies, after receiving our tickets, we just did not walk directly to our seats, and an usher would take our ticket, examine it with a flashlight, and would ask us to follow him. We would walk into the theater behind the usher as the light swiftly passed other seats. We could see, but not where we were going until finally, we reached our seats.

The usher, in this metaphor, is the Holy Spirit, as he leads us to our purpose in life. We can be rebellious and decide to find it on our own (waste a lot of time), or we call to allow God's usher to direct us to our chosen spot. As destiny walks with us, we can hardly see without the guidance of God's usher. Now and then, we could see certain things but not clearly, but we trust the usher and continue to follow until we reach our designated spot. That's the purpose in your life and mine.

Prayer

Lord, I have stumbled and fallen because I would not listen to the signs you gave me about my life over the years. I am sorry for not listening to you, as you have sent signs through my wife, my family, my friends, and my church family. Help me to see more clearly, and help me to act responsibly in finding out my purpose in life. I will always honor you with my life, substance, and faith. Thank you, Lord, (Amen).

CHAPTER-4

Pride

Philippians 2:1-3

King James Version

[2] If there be therefore any consolation in Christ, if any comfort of love, if any fellowship of the spirit, if any bowels and mercies,

[2] Fulfil ye my joy, that ye be likeminded, having the same love, being of one accord, of one mind.

[3] Let nothing be done through strife or vainglory, but in lowliness of mind, let each esteem other better than themselves.

Pride is a feeling of deep pleasure or satisfaction derived from one's achievements, the achievements of those with whom one is closely associated, or from qualities or possessions that are widely admired.

The biblical understanding of pride is quite different from the dictionary definition of pride. I am not speaking of our pride in our children's accomplishments, owning a new car, or the pride we take when others are given honors.

I am talking about the pride that makes us think we can look down on others because of our gifts or funds. Or the pride we have in our family and how the family stands as though they are the only blessed family. Jesus hasn't stopped giving out blessings.

It's that old pride that make another look down on people because of their status in life. In ancient times, when the merchant with all his worldly goods approached the market gate, some things had to be done. First, the gate that the camel had to enter was small. That meant the merchant had to take all the products on the camels and come down through the gate. Then, he had to stoop very low to enter the gate.

The one element to fighting pride is humility and repentance. Contrition (Psalms 51) puts us in a framework of repentance, which means I am totally and completely sorry for how I acted or made you feel. Would you please forgive me?

Humility is the constant reminder that without God, we are nothing, and with Him, we are everything.

Always show gratitude, and show the nation and the world how the Lord changed our bad attitudes and gave us the heart of compassion for others.

Prayer

Lord, sometimes I wake up with an arrogant attitude, as If I am the only person that matters on this planet. I try to show off my ability and worldly goods; you could have knocked me into eternity. I am so sorry for how I treated you and others around me. I am going to do better with your help. Keep my mind focused on the things you have done for me in my life. I don't take you for granted, Lord. I thank you for helping me to turn pride into humility, and arrogance into praise, for you, are worthy of being praised, (Amen)

CHAPTER-5

Temptation

1 Corinthians 10:13

King James Version

[13] There hath no temptation taken you but such as is common to man: but God is faithful, who will not suffer you to be tempted above that ye are able; but will with the temptation also make a way to escape, that ye may be able to bear it.

When I was younger, we lived in a very close neighborhood, and we were close families. One of our neighbors had an apple tree in the backyard. All the children were told to stay away from the apple trees. They gave their reasons; a high wall surrounded the trees, and if you fell, it would hurt; the apples were not ripe, and if we ate them, they would give us a stomach ache.

Those were good reasons to stay away, yet the adventurous, curious little kids we were would not let that stop us from trying. I could see those apples in my hand, the smell, the taste, the challenge. I do it all, except for the noted objection coming from the owner. I was determined to take a chance. One evening I thought I scaled the wall and grabbed some of those apples even though I was told not to.

Several things came into play. The wall was easy, and the apples were plentiful, but the owner let the dog out of the house. I got what I wanted, but I lost what I had. I fell off the fence because I was nervous, hurt my ankle, tore my pants, the dog nipped me on the leg, and to make things worse, the apples made me throw up and go to the bathroom all night. All because I would not listen.

As young adults, your temptations are more complex and have dangerous consequences. You are worried about your house, your bills, your relationship, and all of a sudden, and someone offers you a drink. You don't drink, but today you thought you needed something to ease the pain. Without thinking about it, you take it and another, and that little drink starts you on a journey of alcoholism that, to this day, you are trying to stop. Maybe it is gambling? You perceive yourself as a millionaire because of your winnings, but the more you gamble, the worse your finances become. Or perhaps, you decide your relationship doesn't have enough sparks in it, and you met someone you like to be with. You quietly began a romance outside the house, leading to much heartache and pain.

Perhaps it is medication in the form of pills or habit-forming drugs that has captivated you. Now you are trapped. You can no longer live without them. They are causing depression, loss of self-worth, guilt, and shame.

How to get off these merry-go-rounds? What is the solution to the problem? The scripture says, what you are facing is as old as humanity. There isn't anything new under the sun, says King Solomon.

First, don't try to fool yourself into thinking you can handle it alone. Pray first, and then if it is of a physical or psychological nature, find a good Christian physician to help you. Then, find a helpful, reliable friend that you can confine.

Don't allow the temptations of life to cheat you out of a blessed, fruitful, and productive life. Unfortunately, you have much to fight for.

The enemy of humanity is the prince of darkness; he is happy for your troubles; in fact, he would love to see more trouble in your life. Resist him with all your might, and if you have not accepted Christ as your savior, do it now. He died on the cross so that we may have eternal life but also have life more abundantly (John 10:9-10). If you have accepted heaven's offer but have turned away from Him somehow, you need to restore yourselves to the Lord. He will give you the strength to withstand all the temptations that will come your way.

Prayer

Lord, I am either in temptation now, coming out of temptation, or on my way to temptation. I know you know what I am now facing. It is hard to break away; I am torn in several directions and don't know where to go. But, I need you right at this moment. Outside, it looks like I have everything together, my family, my relationships, my friends, and even my church family. But, inside, I feel empty, lonely, and depressed. Would you make a difference in my life? Would you make the sunshine in my heart again?

Help me to face the temptations. Show me how to resist them and keep me safe; thank you! (Amen).

CHAPTER-6

Laugher

Proverbs 17:22

King James Version

[22] A merry heart doeth good like a medicine: but a broken spirit drieth the bones.

I love this saying, "If laughter is like good medicine, you must take one dose daily!"

Taking your life and yourself seriously every day is dangerous business. To look like you have been sucking on lemons all day is not a good idea. Learn how to relax, enjoy your life, and enjoy your family. Instead of listing all the things you don't have, why not list your blessings? They will surely outweigh all you don't have by a wide margin.

Find something during the day to laugh at, something that does not hurt anyone's feelings but a nice, clean story.

I want to share a story with you. A woman, her friend, said she was always talking about how sick she was and how she would complain about her sickness to everyone she met.

Then, a few months later, she passed away. Her friends attended her funeral and went to the burial grounds to pay final respect. They were beginning to leave after the service, but one stayed to watch the final interment. They placed the tombstone on the ground. He became curious to see what was written on the tombstone. Finally, on the tombstone for all the world to see were her final words, "See, I told you I was sick!"

Every time I think of that story, I have to laugh. But, you find humorous stories that will lift you and make you feel that life is not as bad as you thought. And you will be on the road to recovery.

Give laughter a chance; in a world of mixed, no, and rare emotions, allow laughter a portion of your time before the workday becomes too stressful. If I listed some of the things that laughter will do, they would be:

1. Laughter heals a lot of hurts
2. Laughter transforms attitudes
3. Laughter unifies friends
4. Laughter brings joy to the heart
5. Laughter makes friends out of enemies

6. Laughter brings sunlight into a room
7. Laughter is a blessing from God

Prayer

Lord, we are not laughing to avoid our problems, burdens, sorrows, and hurts. We are laughing despite them. You have allowed us to laugh, and we will take full advantage of this blessing. You are so wise, and yet you are also kind. We thank you for your saving grace and the miraculous power on display in everything we awake. We see your power in the wind and the sun and nature. We see your power in humanity, your zenith of creation. We are in awe of your majestic mountains and oceans. Lord, Just the ability to laugh gives us hope for a brighter day. Thank you. (Amen)

CHAPTER-7

Successful

John 4:30-34

30 Then they went out of the city and came unto him.

31 In the meantime, his disciples prayed to him, saying, Master, eat.

32 But he said unto them, I have meat to eat that ye know not of.

33 Therefore said the disciples one to another, Hath any man brought him ought to eat?

34 Jesus saith unto them, my meat is to do the will of him that sent me and to finish his work.

What would be considered successful? There are many words used to describe

Successful: accomplishment, achievement, advance, benefit, boom, fame, gain, and happiness. We are using the world's metrics as to what success appears to be. I must agree the wording is inviting, and there seem to be elements of a financial nature attached to the wording.

You know of many people who were gifted individuals. They were artists, athletes, actors, and others with promising careers who were labeled successful, who left this world disappointed and sad. Yet, some achieved the same and are also considered successful, with personal testimonies of satisfaction and fulfillment. What makes the difference? I have come to realize over the years that the closer we are to what the Lord wants out of our life, the more we have satisfaction and a sense of fulfillment.

In the scripture, Jesus had just finished speaking with the woman at the well. She was so convinced that the one she spoke to was the Son of God that she told everyone she met, and the whole town came out to see Jesus. May accept the Lord as their savior.

The disciples avoided talking to the woman and the entire town because they were not of the Hebrew family. But thank the Lord that Jesus went straight through the town specifically to speak with this woman who happened to be a Samaritan (half Jew and half gentile). The disciples said to Jesus, "We went out to get meat from the Hebrew butcher shop." Jesus said you brought meat for me, but you don't realize I have a different kind of meat. He said, “My meat is to do the will of Him that sent me.” So Jesus was saying that what feeds me and gives me satisfaction and fulfillment is to do my father’s will.

This should be the conversation of all believers. Considering all the abilities the Lord has given us, we should find a way to use that ability for the glory of God. That is a heavenly description of success. “The Lord did not designate us to be successful and told us to be faithful!

Prayer

Lord, you have planned my life; you have given me abilities for your glory; for this, I am grateful. I know my life is in your hands. I was hoping you could help me to continue the journey and the direction you have placed in my life. May I never bring shame and disgrace on you, but help me testify to your goodness and grace. Like the persons in the Bible, you gave us talents, and I want to give back to you more than you gave me. In Jesus' name, (Amen).

CHAPTER-8

Romans 8:35-39

35 Who shall separate us from the love of Christ? Shall tribulation, distress, persecution, famine, nakedness, peril, or sword?

36 As it is written, For thy sake, we are killed all the day long; we are accounted as sheep for the slaughter.

37 Nay, in all these things, we are more than conquerors through him that loved us.

38 For I am persuaded, that neither death, nor life, nor angels, nor principalities, nor powers, nor things present, nor things to come,

39 Nor height, depth, or any other creature, shall be able to separate us from the love of God, which is in Christ Jesus our Lord.

Distractions

Distractions are horrible. They impede our progress and hinder us from productivity. A thing that prevents someone from giving full attention to something else is a distraction.

It is said that some demons were preparing to influence humans from being saved. The head demon stated: “Who will volunteer to go to earth and tell them there is no heaven!” One demon said, “I will.” He tried and tried, but no results. When asked about his lack of results, he said nearly everybody knows there is a heaven! Another demon stood and said, “I will be a distraction by telling them there is no hell!” He returned as empty and discussed as the first demon, with no results.

Finally, the last demon, “I have a way to bring the best results.” We he returned, there was standing room only. The head demon said, “What did you say to influence these people to come to this place of doom and destruction?” The demon said, unlike my counterparts, I did not tell them there is no heaven, neither did I repeat there is no hell, I just told them, There Is No Hurry”. Thus, no hurry becomes a distraction itself. I can continue my routine: wake up, eat breakfast, go to work, go on vacation, raise the kids, attend graduations and weddings, retire, and leave this world lost. You have been distracted by life, and it is easy to do. Living without much help from heaven because of a fractured relationship with heaven leads to a dismal outcome.

For horses that are easily distracted while racing, the owner permits them to wear blinders. These little instruments are placed around the head and stick closely to the eyes, which causes the horse not to see anything but that which is totally before him.

If the Lord knows every hair on our heads (in my case, every hair that used to be on my head) (Matthew 10:30), then he is fully aware of our distractions and how they affect our lives and our ability to become servants for the Lord.

If we ask Him, he will allow the Holy Spirit to place spiritual blinders on us to carry out the Lord's will for our lives. And what is his will for us? That we would help others to salvation through Jesus Christ.

Prayer

Lord, I find it difficult to focus on my kids' appointments and activities, my job demands, and my wife's obligations. It is a stressful situation that your spirit can only help. Would you calm me down and tell my anxious heart to exhale? Would you assure me that trouble doesn't always last and that the sun always shines somewhere? I need you more than ever! Thank you for my past accomplishments, and I know you will take care of my present situation and future. I trust you, Lord! (Amen).

CHAPTER-9

Acts 4:34-37

34 Neither was there any among them that lacked: for as
many as were possessors of lands or houses sold them and
brought the prices of the things that were sold,

35 And laid them down at the apostles' feet: distribution was
made unto every man according to his need.

36 And Joses, who by the apostles was surnamed Barnabas,
(which is, being interpreted, The son of consolation,) a
Levite, and of the country of Cyprus,

37 Having land, sold it, and brought the money, and laid it at
the apostles' feet.

Encourager

This was the beginning of the church when persecution was just beginning, and over two months, the church grew from a few people in the upper room in Jerusalem to over three thousand people. How will they maintain and sustain this kind of crowd? They probably lose jobs, disowned by family members. They are facing no food to eat and no place to stay. How will their needs be met?

Those that were a part of the Christian movement sold their property and gave it to the leadership to be distributed among the people. Among them was a man named Joses, who had another name: Barnabas. An interesting name. The Greek word (paraklēseōs), from which we receive the word, paramedic. This word means those from the medical profession run to our rescue and transport us to the hospital. Will traveling assist us and keep or maintain our vital signs until we arrive at the hospital?

Barnabus acts in a way to maintain the masses until more financial help can assist them. His name also is "Son of Conciliation," or Son of Encouragement." He does not go around speaking gloom and doom. Instead, he lifts people with positive words. Words that are meaningful and sincere. He was not interested in making a name for himself, just the willingness to help others. Encouragers are of a different breed. They are not jealous of others' productivity; they are happy and express that directly to the person. Encouragers bring life into a room just by their presence. They give support to others because they have compassion for others. They truly know what it is to struggle, but through their struggle, they become stronger and a helper to those who think no one cares about them.

Are you an encourager? If you are congratulations, your life will be more fulfilled and enriched by what you do to help others. You can rest easy at night knowing the sun did not set until you lifted someone's spirit.

Prayer

Lord, it is at these times I feel a little closer to you. I learned that the more I encourage others, the better I feel. It refreshes me in the morning when I awake and places a smile on my face and joy in my heart. Lord, it is all because of you. I am no longer frightened by my past or present and looking forward to my future as long as you are in charge of my life. (amen)

CHAPTER-10

Mentorship

1 John 2:14

King James Version

[14] I have written unto you, fathers, because ye have known him that is from the beginning. I have written unto you, young men, because ye are strong, and the word of God abideth in you, and you have overcome the wicked.

In my profession as a retired senior Pastor, it is important to help train others who will someday become a part of the ministry. It may be a missionary, instructor, Evangelist, or Pastor. Over my lifetime, I helped produce at least 75-100 great leaders in the church. I am not boasting and am humbled by the opportunity to prepare these young people for the task that lies before them.

The young because they are strong, the old because they are aware of which way to go. What a great combination, a great team. Yet, today it is difficult to bring the two groups together. Jealousy and envy create disturbances between the groups, which interrupts their effectiveness, which is very unfortunate because they need each other to be effective. I know each day I can understand what it means to wake up in the morning with less strength, yet my life experiences make up the difference. On the other hand, the young such as yourselves have the energy and strength to accomplish so much if you know the direction to pour your energy. That is why racism is so non-productive because each race has been given talents, but they are non-effective as a group because of old hang-ups about color. Thanks to Christ, the hang-ups are hung up at the cross, and liberation is available there the cross. (…There is neither Jew nor Greek, neither bond nor free, and neither male nor female: for ye is all one in Christ Jesus, (Galatians 3:28).

In your profession, find someone you can mentor and help guide them in a positive direction, for a cemetery is the wrong place to find a Library. We must not leave this world without sharing our gifts and abilities with the Lord.

Prayer

Lord, you are my light and my salvation, my refuge in a time of a storm, and you have done so much for me in my life. You have given me gifts, talents, and abilities, from building a house to hunting in the wilderness, solving math problems, dunking a basketball, and many more. Now, I pour them out to you by mentoring others. I want you to know I appreciate everything you have placed in my hands; I don't take it for granted nor boast, but I will share what you have given me in humility! Thank you, (Amen)

CHAPTER-11

Philippians 4:6-7

Be careful with nothing, but in everything by prayer and supplication with thanksgiving, let your requests be made known unto God. And the peace of God, which passeth all understanding, shall keep your hearts and minds through Christ Jesus.

Prayer

There is no better arsenal to add to your life than prayer. It gives such peace and understanding to our hopes and aspirations, and prayer is the constant and routine communication with our Lord. Prayer is talking to Him as if you were talking to a friend.

Prayer is the ascension of our spirit to find meaning and purpose in a meaningless world. The Lord has granted believers the privileged to commune with him. The Bible is filled with examples of common people like you and me who constantly communed with the Lord.

How much time should I spend with the Lord in Prayer? As much time as you deem necessary. I would suggest you make sure that it is quality time. Do not become distracted by the cell phone, TV, kids, or mentally. Find a place in your home where it is quiet and peaceful to share your burdens. It could be like me, in the morning before everyone is stirring around the house, or in the evening, while others prepare for bed. It will make all the difference in your focus and fulfillment of value in life circumstances. You could pray with your spouse or pray individually. It is said that prayer changes things, and that is true. But it is also true that prayer changes people who make a change in their lives and lifestyles. I want to share with you some quotes about prayer:

"If you believe in prayer, expect God to hear you. If you do not expect, you will not have. God will not hear you unless you believe He will hear you; but if you believe He will, He will be as good as your faith." – Charles Spurgeon

"Prayer should not be regarded as a duty which must be performed, but rather as a privilege to be enjoyed, a rare delight that is always revealing some new beauty." – E.M. Bounds

“God can handle your doubt, anger, fear, grief, confusion, and questions. You can bring everything to him in prayer.” – Rick Warren

“Prayers outlive the lives of those who uttered them; outlive a generation, outlive an age, outlive a world.” – E.M Bounds

54 LIFE CHANGING Prayer Quotes - The Best Of The Best! - The Blazing Center

The scripture says in all things with prayer. There isn’t anything too hard that prayer cannot handle. Supplication means after I realize that our God is capable of answering our prayers, we begin in detail what is needed in our situation and tell the Lord all about it. I always say the Lord answers in three ways: Yes, no, and wait.

Yes, means our prayers and lining up with the will of God. No, our prayer does not align with God's will, for there may be something in that prayer request that might harm us. Wait means it also aligns with God's will, but it is just not the proper time for it to take full fruition.

There is a song entitled: “Sweet hour of Prayer.” This song is over 140 years old, yet it was so miraculously and prayerfully came together. In 1842, the owner William Walford was putting up stock in a little tinker shop in Coleshill, Warwickshire, England. Walford is almost blind. On this day, his friend, Rev Thomas Salmon, came in. Walford asked his friend to copy a poem in his mind (this poem is the words to what we now call "Sweet Hour of Prayer"). The pastor was asked to write the poem down as dictated to him. The poem so impressed the friend that he made two copies, gave one to Walford, and placed one in his pocket. Three years later, Salmon traveled to the United States and sent Walford's poem to the editor of the New York Observer, published on September 13, 1845. The poem also carried the story of Salmon, having received it by dictation from his blind friend.

It was then published in the Baptist Hymnal in 1859 and included in a book called Church Melodies, Published that same year. It was noticed by an American composer of gospel music, William Bradbury, and it was placed to music. The Lord's power and majesty to take a small thought from the mind of a blind store owner, dictated by his friend, then, on a trip to the United States, sends it to an editor, then picked up by a composer. The result is a hymn that has strengthened and encouraged faith on both sides of the Atlantic for many years and continues for years.

Sweet Hour of Prayer

Sweet hour of prayer! Sweet hour of prayer!

That calls me from a world of care,

And bids me at my father's throne

Make all my wants and wishes known.

In seasons of distress and grief,

My soul has often found relief

And oft escaped the tempter's snare

By thy return, sweet hour of prayer!

Sweet hour of prayer! Sweet hour of prayer!

The joys I feel, the bliss I share,

Of those whose anxious spirits burn

With strong desires for thy return!

With such, I hasten to the place

Where God my Savior shows His face,

And gladly take my station there,

And wait for thee, sweet hour of prayer!

Sweet hour of prayer! Sweet hour of prayer!

Thy wings shall my petition bear

To Him whose truth and faithfulness

Engage the waiting soul to bless.

And since He bids me seek His face,

Believe His Word and trust His grace,

I'll cast on Him my every care,

And wait for thee, sweet hour of prayer!

Sweet hour of prayer! Sweet hour of prayer!

May I thy consolation share,

Till, from Mount Pisgah's lofty height,

I view my home and take my flight:

This robe of flesh I'll drop and rise

To seize the everlasting prize;

And shout, while passing through the air,

"Farewell, farewell, sweet hour of prayer!"

Prayer

Lord, sharing my thoughts, failures, and achievements with the universe's creator is precious. Thank you for your visibly seen creative genius, but also for that subtle way you enter our hearts and inspire us in our minds to give to the world what you have impressed upon us. We will honor you and give you glory and praise for your goodness and mercy. In Jesus' name, Amen.

CHAPTER-12

Conformity

[2] And be not conformed to this world: but be ye transformed by the renewing of your mind, that ye may prove what is that good, and acceptable, and perfect, will of God.

As young adults, you know the importance of independence and freedom. You are now on your own (Yet, some are still at home until it gets better for them, job, education, employment, etc.), yet several entities influence you in life; peer groups, friends, fellow students, communications: Facebook, zoom, webinar, Twitter, and so much more.

What should be your position under such pressure in this world? The old preacher, Apostle Paul, states we must be aware of the believers, position in Christ. We must ensure that we are in step with what the kingdom of heaven means to us. Do not let the Bible become just a piece of artwork on the living room lampstand.

Paul reminds us of our responsibility to Christ because of what he has done for us on Calvary. Jesus made the ultimate divine and human sacrifice for us, thus, eliminating and for of condemnation for us because of sin (Romans 8), and is now pointing out what we must do after salvation. The Lord does not want us to collaborate with a world system opposed to heavenly intent and will.

The words are conformity and transformity. Conformity is more passive and stationary in thought. However, transformity is more movement and activity. Conformity has an element in this example. A ready-mix truck arrived at a designated residential home to lay down concrete for a driveway. Once the concrete is poured into the driveway mold and set up, it will remain that way until someone chooses to release it by destroying it.

Paul is saying he does not want us to allow the world to palace us in an irreversible mold so that we are interested in what the world is saying. Paul is said to move from that dismal thinking and begin to refresh your mind upon heavenly things. The scripture says it so much better than I can:

Philippians 4:8

8 Finally, brethren, whatsoever things are true, whatsoever
things are honest, whatsoever things are just, whatsoever

things are pure, whatsoever things are lovely, whatsoever things are of good report; if there be any virtue, and if there be any praise, think on these things, (Philippians 4:8)

Our mind has been renewed, affecting our attitudes, actions, and ability to help God's kingdom.

Prayer

Lord, sometimes this world wears us out. I am being pulled in so many directions. I am not sure about the position I must take. Will you help me through this maze of influence, good or ill, and help me see and think clearly about issues that will make a difference in my life and society? I know you have all power and can keep me from making wrong mistakes. Keep me, place me in your arms and help me to do your will. (Amen)

CHAPTER-13

Confidence

2 Corinthians 1:9-10

[9] Indeed, we felt we had received the sentence of death. But this happened that we might not rely on ourselves but on God, who raises the dead.

[10] He has delivered us from such a deadly peril and will deliver us again. On him, we have set our hope that he will continue to deliver us,

Within human mentality, the definition is quite different from the biblical makeup. For humans, it is the capability to depend upon our ability to make it through any and every situation and circumstance.

What is being inferred is that we can handle any situation that comes to pass. How foolish it is to think, in our capacity, we can make it through everything. There are too many variables that we cannot perceive. We need outside help from another source.

Faith in the Lord and the assurance of salvation through Christ gives us what I call "Holy Boldness" to face many dangers knowing our heavenly father knows and will act on our behalf.

When growing up, there were times I had to face bullies at school. They would take your lunch money and even your tennis shoes. On this particular day, I saw one of them coming my way. I had several options: run past the bully, run away from the bully and deal with him another day, or walk directly to him and face my fears. On this day, I decided to face my fears. As I walked directly toward him, for the first time, I saw fear in his eyes; I said in my mind, "Oh yeah, I've got him on the run; I began to speed up toward him, and he began to slow down, and finally he turned around and ran away. I felt so good inside to know that I had confidence in myself to make a bully run away.

I thought that was great. However, when I turned around, I was surrounded by my brothers; they were there all the time.

Just like my brothers gave me protection, the holy spirit is our protection. That invisible power that we cannot see, working on our behalf. When that old bully (Satan) tries to deceive us, the holy spirit is there to help repel his darts thrown at us. The dart of evil, the dart of discouragement, the dart of deceit and despair, the dart of depression and loneliness, and the dart of sin and hatred all fall to the ground because of his faithfulness to us.

Do not become a victim to Satanic attacks, not a statistic on the stage of a human tragedy, for we are more than conquerors through Him that loved us (Romans 8).

Another example of confidence is examining Jesus's Disciples before Jesus went to the cross and after the cross; there is a difference in their attitude and behavior. Before the cross, Peter told Jesus how he would be the only disciple who would not forsake him. We know how that turned out; it was awful. When the temple guards tried to take Jesus into the garden, Peter awoke, tried to fight with his sword, and cut off one of the Priest aid's ears. Jesus repaired the ear with one touch and told Peter to put up his sword, "He that lives by the sword will perish by the sword."(Matthew 26:52). Peter also stood outside warming by a fire (It probably was cold at night), to hear the court proceedings for Jesus. This was when he was asked if he was one of His disciples; Peter said three times, "I do not know Him." That is when the cock crowed. An awful night it was for Peter. The other disciples went into hiding, except for John. Jesus was crucified that Friday, but a resurrection took place Sunday morning. For forty days, the people could see Jesus, listen to Jesus give His final acclamations and tell his disciples to go and make disciples.

After the resurrection, Peter and the other disciples were no longer afraid and confident that they came straight from heaven. The book of Acts speaks of Peter and the disciples as being men of boldness. Their confidence flowed from the savior. Jesus is alive today, even now.

Prayer

Lord, I have read the stories of others and how you helped them to regain their confidence and increase their boldness. Would you do the same for me? Sometimes, my faith wavers and my confidence isn't as strong as it should be. But I know when I am weak, you are strong. Help me to engage myself in the full assurance that you are with me. I need you more on this day to face my challenges. Thank you in advance. (Amen)

CHAPTER-14

Patience

Isaiah 40:31

King James Version

31 But they that wait upon the Lord shall renew their strength; they shall mount up with wings as eagles; they shall run, not be weary, and they shall walk, and not faint.

Our society and culture are quite different than when I arrived. Then, there was much respect for the elderly; because of their experience and wisdom, they were revered. The children were dismissed from the room when they spoke to other adults.

Today it is said that impatience is a virtue. I had never heard that until this era. Someone said, "I want patience, and I want it now! After all the technology we have, moving information in seconds and cooking food in seconds, we expect our lives to be transformed in seconds. It just doesn't work like that.

A businessman was asked about the key to his enormous success. The businessman said, "failure" the man said, failure? The businessman said yes, for, without failure, I would not know what patience looked like, which led me to experience more failure, which led to my success.

We see the athletes on TV and dream of being one of those unique specimens of grace and ability. However, we never stop to think about what kind of regimen they had to develop, the training, the practice, the running of many miles, the lifting of many weights, the 2 a day in football, the stress and strain, the broken ankles or pulled muscles which eliminate their participation in activities for this year. There is no success with paying the price to achieve.

Patience is not all about waiting; it is about having a great attitude while you wait. Not only is it physically waiting, but having the mental capacity to wait and proceed knowing there is a God that will guide your steps. Did you not know that patience and perseverance are neighbors who work together to make obstacles and difficulties vanish?

Never cut a tree down in the wintertime. Never make a negative decision in the low time. Never make your most important decisions when you are in your worst moods.

Wait. Be patient. The storm will pass. The spring will come. Robert H. Schuller

Read more at https://www.brainyquote.com/topics/patience-quotes

Be patient and understanding. Life is too short to be vengeful or malicious.

Phillips Brooks

Patience and Diligence, like faith, remove mountains.

William Penn

Prayer

Lord, keep me from falling in the category of the impatient. I am willing to wait on you, for you know my blueprint for my life. Keep me quiet while I wait for your hand of perseverance to move into my life. Keep my mind and heart clear of sinful thoughts while I wait. Surround me with peers that understand the importance of patience. May the voice I only hear be yours. (Amen)

CHAPTER-15

Grateful

1 Thessalonians 5:16-18. Rejoice always, pray continually, and give thanks in all circumstances, for this is God's will for you in Christ Jesus.

I was in the third grade when our house in Akron, Ohio, was on fire. It was a cold winter night; I could hear the fire trucks as they arrived. Our neighbors grabbed a ladder, and we escaped from the roof. That night I learned what being grateful was all about. Our neighbor allowed us into their home, and I remember our pastor visiting us to pray and encourage us.

My third-grade class at Robinson Elementary taught me what sharing and caring looked like. They brought my class clothcs, toys, and much more for my family. I was so grateful; I was taken to each class so I could express my appreciation to all my schoolmates.

Look over your life, family, job, or profession. Consider your health and the health of your family and friends. You are mobile and don't need to be carried or a wheelchair (still possible). Your finances are in order, and your children are not in jail or prison (hopefully). That is enough to be grateful. Do not dwell upon that which is negative. It will leave you helpless, hopeless, and without strength. Instead, dwell upon being grateful, your happiness will increase, and your sense of well-being will be enhanced. We never appreciate what we have until we no longer have it.

There was a doctor who had been practicing for many years. It was easy to tell his patients about their pain and their disposition. He spoke it with so much ease and professionalism until one day, and the doctor needed surgery. From that moment to the end of his professional career, he developed an attitude of compassion for those who experienced what he experienced. Don't take your life for granted and the people who love and care for you. Be grateful!

Prayer

Lord, it is so easy to live our lives as if it was normal that we would receive daily benefits until it is taken away. Our pride turns to dust, our arrogance flies away, and we are left with emptiness. Lord, help us to be aware of the importance of time in our lives and teach us to have the ability to be patient and, above all, grateful for everything you have done in my life. (Amen)

CHAPTER-16

Finances

Psalms 24:1

The earth is the Lord's, and the fulness thereof; the world, and they that dwell therein.

How to keep the right perspective on finances in a world that judges individuals based on what they have? This is a difficult subject to tackle, but it is needful to have a well-rounded life. So how do you stay grounded with an enormous amount of finance, and how do you not be overwhelmed by the lack of finance?

Young adults starting will have problems adjusting from single life to married life. In your single life, you were your financier. You had no accountability problems because, being single, you bought whatever you wanted. Now, with a marriage partner, it is quite different. Who will handle the finances? Make a definitive decision because many break-ups begin and end with finances.

The priority position in our finances must consider the following, "Who is the Landlord over my finances, and

Who is the Tenant?". In this illustration, the Lord is the Landlord, and we are the tenants over our finances. Everything we think we own belongs to another. One hundred years from this date, it will not matter what house we lived in, what cars we have driven, or even how much was in our checking and saving accounts, for one life will be passed, but only what we do for Christ will last.

The Pauline epistle is saturated with the idea of moderation in our approach to life, which includes clothes, food, our choice of house, cars, and finance. I heard one individual say, "It's not how much one makes; it's how much we keep! If your debt is much lower than your weekly paycheck, and you remain constant with your finances, baring no surprises, you will always be left with a surplus.

One thing I found so difficult for young adults is giving to their place of worship. They feel there is no need to give when they arrive; the lights are on, the sanctuary seems clean, the air is on during the summer, and the heat is on. Everyone is happy and filled with spirit.

The question is, how do you think those things are functioning without your participation and finances?

Learning to be good stewards of what the Lord has given us leads to more blessings that you cannot imagine; good health, a sense of wellness and wholeness, blessings upon your family, your children, blessings on your job, your finances, and so many more. (Malachi 3:10):

[10] Bring ye all the tithes into the storehouse, that there may be meat in mine house, and prove me now herewith, saith the Lord of hosts, if I will not open you the windows of heaven, and pour you out a blessing, that there shall not be room enough to receive it.

There was a story about a Christian farmer who had learned to become a good steward over the things the Lord left in his hands over the years. Upon interview, he was asked the secret of his great wealth and prosperity. He responded, “It’s very simple; around the farm are many tools, one of them is the shovel, you see, I shovel to the Lord, and the lord shovel back to me, and you know his shovel is a lot bigger than my shovel!

I did not say it would be easy; sometime you will succeed, and sometime you will fail, but in the failing, press toward consistency, and it will become automatic in your life. Then, finally, you will look back over your life (for the years will fly) and will be glad you followed the principle found in this holy section.

Prayer

Lord, I know you are in charge of everything, the world, and everything in it, including me and all my finances. Sometimes it is hard to figure out and balance my job, my family, my children and their schedule, my wife, and my finances. I know you can handle my problems, but I know I am responsible. Lord, keep my mind clear and my heart open to hear your voice as I carry out my duties financially. I don't want to be so frugal that I eliminate any contribution to the poor and the church. Help me to find a well-balanced approach to life circumstances and my finances. (Amen)

CHAPTER-17

Addiction

Genesis 9:19-21

John 5

[19] These are the three sons of Noah: and of them was the whole earth overspread.

[20] And Noah began to be a husbandman, and he planted a vineyard:

[21] And he drank the wine, and was drunken, and he was uncovered within his tent.

Addiction comes in many forms and many ways. The progression is frightening upon one's tolerance. One can start with a determination not to become involved in anything that appears to be addicting, but after a while, you begin occasional drinking of wine. Then life pressures face you, and you go from casual to serious drinker. Then it begins to get worse from that point. Finally, a broken marriage or relationship becomes the key to your demise. It moves from bad to worse. Now, you cannot have a reasonable day without a drink (It's the same for drugs and other addictive substances).

Addiction is so devastating; it turns professionals into helpless individuals. If you find yourself in this condition, seek the proper help.

Even Noah, the man of God, found himself in an addiction (the fact or condition of being addicted to a particular substance, thing, or activity). Noah's addiction created problems between the brothers, Shem, Ham, and Japheth. How many households across this nation have come under this dilemma? Families torn apart over what kind of solution should be tried? It is a global epidemic.

In John chapter 5, a lame man sits at Bethesda pool. He was carried to that same location for thirty-eight years. When Jesus passed by, he asked this man, "Will thou be made whole?" From this question comes an important point of discussion, as much as we love our loved ones and want them to be totally and completely free of the addiction, nothing can be done until the person realize they need help. That becomes the catalyst for the road to recovery. There must be a "Want to" attitude. It is not an easy journey, but it has been accomplished with professional help and prayer.

addiction definition – Google Search

Prayer

Lord, this is a very difficult part of my life. I don't know how to begin on behalf Of my loved one. (Or myself). Lord, I have never faced something like this; it is different. I have seen so much in the last few years that is discouraging and overwhelming. I need your help; I need your guidance and provision. I have looked over the life of your servant Noah, and I have heard your voice as you spoke to the lame man and asked him if he wanted to be made whole. I know the answer is within you, but there is something I need to do. I need to want a change in my life and help my loved ones conclude that they need a change in their life. Well, you lead me to the right people with the right ability to help me (My family member) regain our health and strength? I cast all my cares upon you, for I know you care for me. Thank you! (Amen)

CHAPTER-18

Regret

Psalms 51

51 Have mercy upon me, O God, according to thy lovingkindness: according unto the multitude of tender mercies blot out my transgressions.

2 Wash me thoroughly from mine iniquity and cleanse me from my sin.

3 For I acknowledge my transgressions: and my sin is ever before me.

4 Against thee, thee only, have I sinned, and done this evil in thy sight: thou mightest be justified when thou speakest and be clear when thou judgest.

Regret deals with past decisions that caused much sorrow and despair or past things that did not turn out as we wished. The Hebrew word for regret is "Sigh," a sort of emotional declaration of past failures, even wasting time in the past.

A past love that has dissolved, a past job you let go of. Maybe it wasn't a relationship or a love, and maybe it was words that were said that did much harm to many people. Looking back over the past, there is regret for saying those words.

The words in Psalms 51 are from one of the greatest, if not the greatest, kings of ancient Israel, King David. He was faithful for most of his life and was considered a man after God's heart. David loved God and praised him through his writings. But, on this particular regret, David transgressed the Law of God.

David regretted the scandal he brought to the palace of Israel and his household. The embarrassment, the humiliation because of his pride. In David's past lies the remorse because he lusted for a married woman. David wanted her even though she was married. David and this woman (Bathsheba) produce a baby. David tries human avenues to alleviate his problems without listening to the voice of God. First, he allows her husband to be killed in battle, and then he marries Bathsheba to cover up the remorse and the regret. Finally, one of God's prophets was sent by God to confront David (Nathan). David finally sees the era of his ways, now, David sees all his sin, and he regrets what was done. Yet, the consequences of his actions are devastating. The baby produced by David and Bathsheba is not allowed to live, David's joy of salvation is gone, and trouble will be in his household until his death.

He asked for forgiveness and was granted, yet he regrets having his way simply because he was king.

What are your regrets of the past that have baffled your mind all these years? There need to be a healing of the memory. It is not only a relationship of a love interest but a love-hate relationship with our parents. They may be departed from this life; you can still have a healing of the memory. If they are still alive, you must tell them and help alleviate this problem in your life so that you can go on with your life in peace.

Prayer

Lord, in these difficult and hard devotionals, I find myself in the middle, not knowing whether to laugh or to cry. My heart is heavy from my past choices; some were good, others were not so good. They spring forth from an immature young person; I was foolish. I know I hurt some people, and in turn, they hurt me as well. I regret the way I acted, and now, I ask for your forgiveness for those things in my past that were not too pleasing to you. As David would say, "Restore unto me, the Joy that come from knowing I am saved," and help me to finish my forgiveness to those who I have offended in my past with the healing of the memories (a prayer for those living or deceased that I have hurt over the years). I love you, Lord, and I trust you will see me through all these circumstances (Amen).

CHAPTER-19

Friends

Proverbs 18:24

24 A man that hath friends must make himself friendly: and there is a friend that sticks closer than a brother.

Friendship is a special gift given to believers by the Lord. (James 1:17). It is a delight to receive this gift. It will help the believer through difficult and blessed days.

There is a difference between friends and associates. Friends do not change sides based on conditions, and associates look for advantages and benefits. Therefore, choose friends wisely, for they can determine your condition and attitude later in life.

What to look for in friends? Compatibility and sometimes contrast. Some things you agree on are part of your convictions, but you may also vary to the end of the spectrum. That is ok if it is perceived as a positive relationship entity. If you are spiritual and excited about your position as a believer in Christ, one needs friends with that same strength, helping each other through reading the Bible, workshops, and study.

Look for friends that will be honest with their assessments of certain things in your life. Of course, I do not always agree with you, but explaining why this certain segment of your life will not work. Honesty, even though it sometimes hurts, is truly the best policy.

A true friend wants you to achieve as high as you can achieve. They are not selfish with friendship and try to block you from other friendships that bloom. They are not intimidated by others but will allow maturity and growth.

A true friend will take the time to pray for you. This is so important in a world of inconsistency and hesitancy to act and react, and it is refreshing to find a friend that would take time on your behalf to express your concerns to the Lord.

A true friend is loyal. This is a major entity within the friendship. You must rely on and trust your friendship to the point where the confidential conversation will be shared and held in safekeeping. I am not speaking of nefarious acts or deeds, but those things that are only sensitive to you and your friend.

True friends are those who can forgive. The reason why pencils are made with erasers is that someone knows that mistakes will be made. There are no complete and perfect friendships. It takes time, but to have a friend willing to forgive, or you are willing to forgive, is Christlike.

True friends do not engage in creating a toxic atmosphere of anger and hate. Instead, they emulate the words of our Lord… "Blessed are the peacemakers, for they shall be called the children of God." It is so easy to destroy relationships, but it takes a caring person to take time to find a way for a friendship to flourish.

Are you the kind of person that others would consider their friend? Can you be trusted with friendship? Are you loyal and faithful? Only you can answer that question. Yet, there is a blessing for those who become a friend and embrace friendship.

Prayer

Lord, you have exposed me to so many elements of friendship, some I was aware of, and some I wasn't aware of. It made me re-evaluate my friends, myself, and my friend. I need your guidance in choosing my friends and keeping the proper friends. I know the scripture is not just speaking of earthly friends; divine friendship for Jesus is the best friend anyone could have. Thank you for being my friend. I will hold your friends near and dear to my heart. (Amen)

CHAPTER-20

Thoughtfulness

Philippians 2:3

King James Version

3 Let nothing be done through strife or vainglory, but in lowliness of mind, let each esteem other better than themselves.

Thoughtfulness runs in juxtaposition to our culture and the attitude of our society. The term is narcissism- excessive interest in or admiration of oneself and one's physical appearance. I would include a pre-occupation with one's life, that it has no room for others' cares or concerns.

It is a disturbing element that does not give room for compassion, helpfulness, concern, and public service. For it becomes "I" instead of "We."

Those with thoughtfulness characteristics bring an honorable gift to our society. They are the ones, despite the littering, who constantly pick up trash on the streets and elsewhere, help the homeless, give to St Jude, or donate to the Salvation army. They care about others and anticipate service where it is needed. The opposite of selfishness and service, a thoughtful element of helping.

Lucy Campbell, a great gospel writer of many songs, wrote an inspirational song that brings full focus on thoughtfulness and service to humanity. Lucy Campbell was notable in the National Baptist Convention U.S.A. Inc, and a global ambassador for the gospel of Jesus Christ. The lyrics capture the sentiment of our theme in this devotional, entitled:

“He Understands, He’ll Say, ‘Well Done”

If when you give the best of your service,

Telling the world that the savior comes;

Be not dismayed when men don’t believe you;

He understands; He’ll say, “Well done.”

Refrain:

Oh, when I come to the end of my journey,

Weary of life and the battle is won;

Carrying the staff and cross of redemption,

He'll understand and say, "Well done."

Prayer

Lord, sometimes I find myself among those that are considered selfish. I concentrate on myself in search of myself. I know this is not what you want out of my life. I need your guidance to help me stimulate my thoughtfulness for others. Make me more like you every day. Change my self-center focus to a Christ-center focus. Help me care more for my family, my church, and others that are non-related. Create a clean heart and renew the right spirit within me (Psalms 51). I will give you the praise, the honor, and the glory, (Amen)

CHAPTER-21

Children

Psalm 127:3-5 ESV

Behold, children are a heritage from the Lord, the fruit of the womb a reward. Like arrows in the hand of a warrior are the children of one's youth. Blessed is the man who fills his quiver with them! He shall not be ashamed when speaking with his enemies at the gate.

My father, who pastored for over 30 years and is now in heaven, said to me in my younger years as he held our first baby in his arms, he said, "Son, cherish these early years because when they are young, sometimes they get on your nerves, but when they are older, they get on your heart." How true is that statement? With young adults today is the question of timing. Of course, you and your spouse have booming professions and want to wait on children. But, then, how do you adjust when the children arrive? What about child care and that all-important entity, the adjustment of children's schedules compared to yours?

All of these elements must be taken into consideration. From a father who has come through this period in my life, along with my wife, it is a very intensive, responsible, all-hands-on-deck period in your life. Yet, before you know it, the time has passed, and you made it through. They will be on their own (if they don’t come back home to live for a while). You will have fond memories of that time in their lives and your life.

In a society where kids are being raised on TV time, TV dinners, and Baby Sitters, you become a vital piece of your children's life. You train, direct, correct, feed, clothe, drive, lift, wipe, care, share, and so much more.

Here are a few quotes from Parents to Children:

1. Butterflies have wings so that they can fly. Bunnies have legs so that they can hop and run. Fish have gills so that they can swim. I have a heart so that I can love you.
2. As a mother, I make mistakes. I am not perfect. And sometimes, I go a little crazy. But all that is okay because I know that no one could ever love my baby the way I do.

3. My baby may not get everything they want in life, but they can be sure they have a mother who loves them unconditionally, more than anything on earth.
4. I love my children because they complete my world with laughter and joy, and I wish for nothing more.
5. My dear children, if you can see yourselves through my eyes, you will see how special you are.
6. A baby will make your days shorter, love stronger, bankroll smaller, clothes shabbier, home happier, the past is forgotten, and the future worth living for.
7. If I could give my baby three things, it would be the strength to follow their passion, the confidence always to know their self-worth, and the ability to know how deeply and truly loved they are.
8. Without my children, my wallet would be full, and my house would be clean, but my heart would be empty and sad.
9. A child may outgrow your lap, but they will never outgrow the love you have in your heart.
10. No matter what, I want my babies to know that they were longed for, wished for, prayed for, and they are forever loved

[50 Beautiful Love Quotes from Parents to Their Children (firstcry.com)]

Prayer

Lord, you have placed in my heart a yearning for children. They have arrived, and now my prayer is answered. You did not tell me how hard it is to raise them. Sometimes I have enough energy; sometimes, my energy wains, and I am left in a moment of depression. When this occurs, you always find a way to lift my burden for the day and make everything alright. The finances might be strained because of unexpected bills for the kids, but you are always there to give me relief. Thank you for your faithfulness in the life of my family. May my memories of my children remain a precious time and one of the most rewarding periods of my life and my spouse. (Amen)

CHAPTER-22

Mask

Exodus 34:33

Exodus 34:33-35

New International Version

[33] When Moses finished speaking to them, he put a veil over his face. 34 But whenever he entered the Lord's presence to speak with him, he removed the veil until he came out. And when he came out and told the Israelites what he had commanded, 35 they saw his face was radiant. Then Moses would put the veil back over his face until he went in to speak with the Lord.

The reason for the mask over Moses's face is the radiance that comes from being in the presence of the Lord. It does not mean that the nation was opposed to God; it was such a frightening experience, an awesome sight that they physically could not face such radiance. For example, think of a glorious summer day. The sun is at its peak of radiance. You look at the sun, but not for long because of the light and radiance. Now, imagine you are looking at the one who is not only radiant but the creator of the radiance of the sun. That is overwhelming.

Moses shields his face because of the over-radiance which emanates from a holy God. On the other hand, why do we humans wear masks? Our masks sometimes are defense mechanisms that shield our emotions and the inner workings of our lives. Our mask becomes our protection from other people and other groups. We are expected to act a certain way, and men are expected not to cry, yet we have things in our lives that make us cry daily. Women are expected to act and react a certain way but careful not to fix in a mold that is not a blueprint of God's will for their lives.

Learn to take away the mask, be true to yourselves and allow the real you to be seen. It feels very refreshing to reveal the true you, and there is no pretension, hypocritical intentions, or inference. You are free to be you!

Prayer

Lord, the mask is cumbersome and out of step with my spiritual life. The mask makes me hide from my friends. It makes them feel like they are not a part of my inner self. I want people close to me. Time is short, so Lord, allow my prayer to come to fruition. I will feel better about myself and the way I represent you. (Amen)

CHAPTER-23

COVID

Isaiah 53:5

5 But he was wounded for our transgressions and bruised for our iniquities: the chastisement of our peace was upon him, and with his stripes, we are healed.

There hasn't been a household or knowing a family that has not been affected by this disease. Even today, the repercussions are still affecting globally. Our hearts are filled with sorrow over the loss of loved ones, those close to us, and those at a distance.

There are many reasons for this disease as it plagues our world. I am not going to entertain any of these at this point. However, I can say Biblically that there is a word to be said for believers who are not faithful to the cause of Christ. Those who have gone so far as to replace the Lord, with another God, such as an increase in amusement, and personal enjoyment, with the lack of church attendance and spiritual growth and maturity. Football, Basketball, and Socker have become the new deity in the life of society.

Let us not fall for the trap of amusement but place a tight grip upon our faith. II Chronicles 7:14 should be the battle cry of all Christians:

2 Chronicles 7:14

King James Version

14 If my people, called by my name, shall humble themselves, pray, seek my face, and turn from their wicked ways; then will I hear from heaven, forgive their sin, and heal their land.

The scripture says we all need to be saved, which is explained in Isaiah 53, because of Christ, we are healed, body, soul, and spirit. But II Chronicles shows us what happens when we behave, our land is healed, our crops return from a draught, and our bodies will no longer need a mask to shield us from diseases. So may we look to our source of healing, clarity, forgiveness, and salvation through our Lord, Christ Jesus.

Lord, our society has sold out to the pleasures, passions, and amusements this world offers; we are addicted to our self-worth. The role we play in helping others has decreased each year. Wake up our sleeping churches and help us to fulfill the great commission. We love you, Lord! In Jesus's name, (Amen)

<-END->

BIBLIOGRAPHY

1. Clinical depression - Google Search
2. The distance of judah to beersheba - Google Search
3. Rest for the body - Google Search
4. Pride definition - Google Search
5. Quotes on laughter is the best medicine - Google Search
6. Successful - Google Search
7. Distractions definition - Google Search
8. Meaning of the name barnabas in the Bible - Google Search
9. Encouragers definition - Google Search
10. 63 Bible Verses about Prayer - KJV - dailyverses.net
11. 54 LIFE CHANGING Prayer Quotes - The Best Of The Best! - The Blazing Center
12. Sweet Hour of Prayer Hymn - William Walford (christianity.com)
13. Confidence Definition and Meaning - Bible Dictionary (biblestudytools.com)
14. Patience Quotes - brainyquote
15. Addiction definition - Google Search
16. What does the Bible say about dealing with regrets? | gotquestions.org
17. Friends in the bible kjv - Google Search
18. 10 Qualities of Godly Friend - Rachel Prochnow
19. Narcissism definition - Google Search
20. Discipleship Ministries | History of Hymns: 'He Understands, He'll... (umcdiscipleship.org)
21. What Does the Bible Say About Children? (openbible.info)

www.ingramcontent.com/pod-product-compliance
Lightning Source LLC
LaVergne TN
LVHW050325160826
845677LV00014B/3540

* 9 7 9 8 8 4 7 6 7 7 1 1 0 *